Dear Parents and Educators,

Welcome to Penguin Young Readers! As parents and educators, you know that each child develops at his or her own pace—in terms of speech, critical thinking, and, of course, reading. Penguin Young Readers recognizes this fact. As a result, each Penguin Young Readers book is assigned a traditional easy-to-read level (1–4) as well as a Guided Reading Level (A–P). Both of these systems will help you choose the right book for your child. Please refer to the back of each book for specific leveling information. Penguin Young Readers features esteemed authors and illustrators, stories about favorite characters, fascinating nonfiction, and more!

Maxed Out!
Gigantic Creatures from the Past

LEVEL 3

GUIDED READING LEVEL **L**

This book is perfect for a **Transitional Reader** who:
- can read multisyllable and compound words;
- can read words with prefixes and suffixes;
- is able to identify story elements (beginning, middle, end, plot, setting, characters, problem, solution); and
- can understand different points of view.

Here are some **activities** you can do during and after reading this book:
- Comprehension: After reading the book, answer the following questions:
  - How tall was an indricotherium? How much did it weigh?
  - Which animal could eat an entire tree, piece by piece?
  - What does the name *basilosaurus* mean?
  - How long was an archelon, the largest turtle ever?
  - Why did the dimetrodon have two types of teeth, one short and one long?
  - Which animal was one of the first things to live on planet Earth?
- Compare/Contrast: In this book, the author says that some of these giant animals looked like animals we see today, only bigger. Using facts from this story, compare and contrast one animal in the book with an animal alive today.

Remember, sharing the love of reading with a child is the best gift you can give!

—Bonnie Bader, EdM
Penguin Young Readers program

*Penguin Young Readers are leveled by independent reviewers applying the standards developed by Irene Fountas and Gay Su Pinnell in *Matching Books to Readers: Using Leveled Books in Guided Reading*, Heinemann, 1999.

To Bonnie Bader, Lana Jacobs, and Sarah Stern (and the Grosset & Dunlap editorial/art team) for their dedication to creating fun, fact-filled books for kids—GLC

To Caden. I hope to hear you read this someday—PM

PENGUIN YOUNG READERS
Published by the Penguin Group
Penguin Group (USA) LLC, 375 Hudson Street, New York, New York 10014, USA

USA | Canada | UK | Ireland | Australia | New Zealand | India | South Africa | China

penguin.com
A Penguin Random House Company

Penguin supports copyright. Copyright fuels creativity, encourages diverse voices, promotes free speech, and creates a vibrant culture. Thank you for buying an authorized edition of this book and for complying with copyright laws by not reproducing, scanning, or distributing any part of it in any form without permission. You are supporting writers and allowing Penguin to continue to publish books for every reader.

Text copyright © 2010 by Ginjer L. Clarke. Illustrations copyright © 2010 by Pete Mueller.
All rights reserved. First published in 2010 by Grosset & Dunlap, an imprint of Penguin Group (USA) LLC.
Published in 2014 by Penguin Young Readers, an imprint of Penguin Group (USA) LLC,
345 Hudson Street, New York, New York 10014. Manufactured in China.

Library of Congress Control Number: 2009020276

ISBN 978-0-448-44827-5   10 9 8 7 6 5 4 3

PENGUIN YOUNG READERS

LEVEL 3
TRANSITIONAL READER

Maxed Out!
Gigantic Creatures from the Past

by Ginjer L. Clarke
illustrated by Pete Mueller

Penguin Young Readers
An Imprint of Penguin Group (USA) LLC

Many gigantic creatures lived millions of years ago. Were they all dinosaurs?

No! There were many different kinds of big beasts. Some of these giants looked like animals we know today—but much, much bigger.

Smilodon (say: SMI-le-don) was a saber-toothed tiger. It attacked and ate animals much larger than itself. It pounced on a bison and knocked it down with its paws. Then smilodon jabbed the bison in the neck with its long fangs. *Ouch!*

Let's check out some more maxed-out monsters!

Chapter 1
Massive Mammals

Indricotherium (say: in-DRIK-oh-THEE-ree-um) was the largest land mammal. It was 25 feet tall—higher than most houses! It weighed at least 20 tons—more than three killer whales!

Indricotherium stretched up to reach the leaves in the treetops. It looked like a rhinoceros with long legs and a giraffe neck. It did not have horns to fight, but it did not need any. Other animals did not mess with this king of the beasts.

Brontotherium (say: BRON-tuh-THEE-ree-um) was smaller than indricotherium but bigger than today's rhinos.

Male brontotheres had unusual Y-shaped horns on their faces. They probably used the horns to fight one another to be in charge.

Boom! Two brontotheres battled with their horns. They rammed each other until one of them got hurt and ran away in defeat. These colossal creatures were called "thunder beasts."

Deinotherium (say: DINE-oh-THEE-ree-um) was larger than today's elephants but looked a lot like one. It had short tusks that curved downward from its lower jaw. Most elephants have long tusks near their trunks that point up.

Craaack! Deinotherium used its sharp tusks to rip off tree bark. This megamammal ate only leaves, bark, roots, and grass. It was an herbivore (say: ER-buh-voor). But deinotherium ate a lot. It could pull a tree into pieces and eat the whole thing!

Megatherium (say: meg-ah-THEE-ree-um) was a giant ground sloth. Like today's tree sloths, megatheres were slow. But they were 10 times bigger than today's sloths—up to 20 feet long.

Megatherium sat on its strong back legs and tail. It held on to a tree trunk with its sharp claws to reach high up in the trees.

Slurrp! It used its long tongue to pull leaves into its mouth and chewed with its back teeth.

Andrewsarchus (say: an-droo-SARK-us) was probably the largest meat-eating mammal that ever lived on land.

It was a carnivore (say: CAR-nuh-voor). It looked like a cross between a big tiger and a dangerous wolf. It was bigger than a bear.

Pow! Andrewsarchus pounced on a small, deerlike animal and knocked it down quickly. It attacked with its huge jaws and large, fearsome teeth. What a mean-looking mammal!

Chapter 2
Colossal Sea Creatures

Basilosaurus (say: BASS-il-oh-SAW-rus) was an immense whale. It grew around 80 feet long. That is the length of a basketball court!

The name *basilosaurus* means "king of the reptiles." People thought it was a dinosaur because its bones were so big. But it lived long after dinosaurs.

Basilosaurus swam by paddling with its front limbs and steering with its huge tail.

Munch! Basilosaurus gobbled fish with its small, jagged teeth. It also ate other sea mammals. That is a mega sea monster!

Carcharodon megalodon (say: car-CAR-oh-don MEG-uh-low-don) was the largest shark ever. It looked like a great white shark, but it was twice as big—more than 50 feet long!

The name *megalodon* means "big tooth." Just one carcharodon tooth was bigger than your hand!

Carcharodon was so enormous that it ate anything it wanted. It even hunted giant whales. This shark ruled the sea!

Elasmosaurus (say: eh-LAZZ-mo-SAW-rus) was a massive water reptile. It was more than 40 feet long. It had a fat body and flippers like a sea turtle. But its thin, snakelike neck was much longer than its body. Its name means "ribbon lizard."

Elasmosaurus could catch fast fish by being sneaky. It held its head up high and waited for fish to swim by. Then it swung its long neck down in the water and grabbed the fish. *Snap!* Its small head was full of ferocious teeth.

Dunkleosteus (say: dunk-lee-OWE-stee-us) was the largest fish ever. It grew up to 30 feet long. It had thick plates on its body, so nothing could hurt it. Dunkleosteus was called the "terror of the seas," because it was a killer fish.

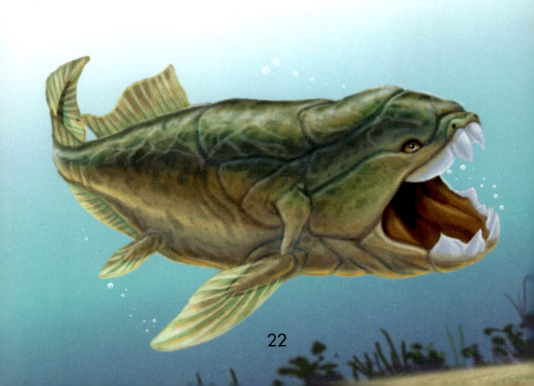

Dunkleosteus did not have teeth. It had hard plates in its mouth that were like a razor-sharp beak.

Chomp! Its bite was very strong. Dunkleosteus fish even attacked each other!

Archelon (say: AR-kuh-lahn)
was the largest turtle ever.
Its name means "king turtle."
It grew at least 12 feet long.
That is the size of a small car!
It looked like a giant sea turtle,
but it had a soft shell.

Archelon could not hide inside its soft shell like most turtles. It paddled in the water with its large flippers.

Snap! Archelon caught a jellyfish in its beak. What a super snapper!

Chapter 3
Giant Reptiles and Birds

Deinosuchus (say: DIE-noh-SOOK-us) was the largest crocodile ever. It grew about 40 feet long. That is more than twice as big as today's crocodiles.

The word *deinosuchus* means "terrible crocodile."

Deinosuchus lurked in the river. It waited for an animal to come to the water's edge to drink.

Slam! Suddenly, it jumped out. It grabbed the surprised creature in its massive jaws and then dragged it back into the river.

Deinosuchus was so huge, it may have even hunted dinosaurs!

Dimetrodon (say: dy-MET-ro-don) was a giant lizardlike animal that lived long before dinosaurs.

It was about 12 feet long, but it looked even bigger. It had a spiked sail on its back that was made of skin stretched over long bones, like a bird's wing. Scientists are not sure what this sail was used for.

Dimetrodon attacked a group of smaller lizards. It moved fast and had teeth as sharp as knives.

The name *dimetrodon* means "two kinds of teeth." It had both short teeth and long teeth in its huge jaws to eat both plants and animals. It was an "omnivore" (say: OM-nuh-voor).

Quetzalcoatlus (say: KWET-zal-KO-at-lus) was a giant reptile that flew. The name *quetzalcoatlus* means "feathered serpent."

It was the largest flying creature. It had a wingspan of about 40 feet, and its body was 25 feet long. That is bigger than some airplanes!

Quetzalcoatlus soared in the air and looked for food below. *Swoop!* It dove down for dinner. It mostly ate dead dinosaurs. Scientists think it was probably a scavenger, like a vulture. Scavengers eat only dead animals.

Argentavis (say: ar-jen-TAH-vis) was the largest bird ever. Its wingspan was 25 feet wide, and it was five feet tall.

It looked like a vulture, but its body was the size of an adult human. It was at least twice as big as the largest birds today.

Argentavis was too big to take off from the ground. It had to get a running start down a hill to fly into the air.

Whoosh! Argentavis dove down and grabbed a big rodent in its sharp, hooked beak. What a fierce flyer!

Diatryma (say: die-uh-TRY-muh) was called a "terror bird." Diatryma could not fly at all because it was so big. It was at least seven feet tall and weighed more than 300 pounds.

Diatryma had a big, curved beak and an enormous head. It probably ate small horses! It ran fast on its long legs and scooped up a horse in a single bite of its beak. That is a scary-looking bird!

Chapter 4
Big, Bad Bugs

Arthropleura (say: ARE-throw-PLUR-ah) was a huge creepy crawler. It was a giant millipede. The word *millipede* means "thousands of feet."

Some of today's millipedes are about one foot long. Arthropleura grew to be at least six feet long!

Arthropleura moved quickly along the forest floor. It probably mostly ate plants, but it might have eaten insects and small animals, too.

Arthropleura had no enemies on land that could break through its hard shell. What a maximum millipede!

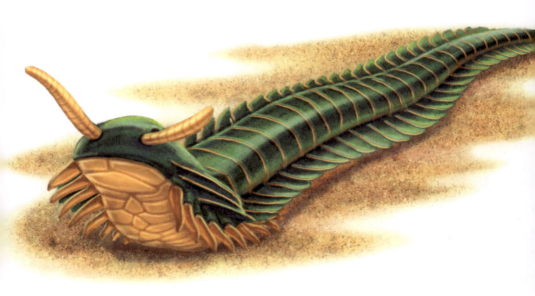

Meganeura (say: meg-a-NOOR-a) was probably the largest insect ever to fly.

It looked like today's dragonflies, but it was much bigger. Its wings were 30 inches wide. That is about as long as an adult human's arm and hand!

Meganeura was so big that it could eat any other insect and even small lizards.

Zoom! It flew down fast and grabbed a giant cockroach in its sticky, spiny legs. It trapped the roach with its big mouthparts and zipped off.

Giant ants were called *Formicium giganteum* (say: for-MISS-ee-um jy-GAN-tee-um). They were the largest ants ever. Giant worker ants were up to one inch long, and their queen was twice as big.

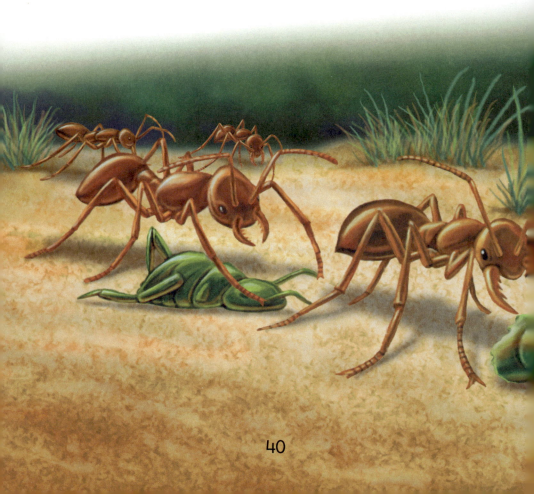

Giant ants lived in huge groups.
They worked together as a team
to eat everything in their path.
These ants even crawled all over
animals and tore them into pieces.
That is an awesome ant army!

Eurypterid (say: yur-IP-ter-id) was a supersize sea scorpion. It grew up to seven feet long. Some eurypterids may even have been twice that big. They lived millions of years ago, when our planet was young.

Eurypterid swam in the ocean using its back legs as paddles. It was covered in armor, and some had a stinging tail.

Snap! It grabbed a large bug with its curved front pincers. Then it trapped the bug in its four pairs of small legs and crunched it into bits.

Trilobites (say: TRY-loh-bites) were one of the first things to live on this planet. They grew up to two feet long and swam on the ocean floor. They looked like horseshoe crabs and weighed up to 10 pounds.

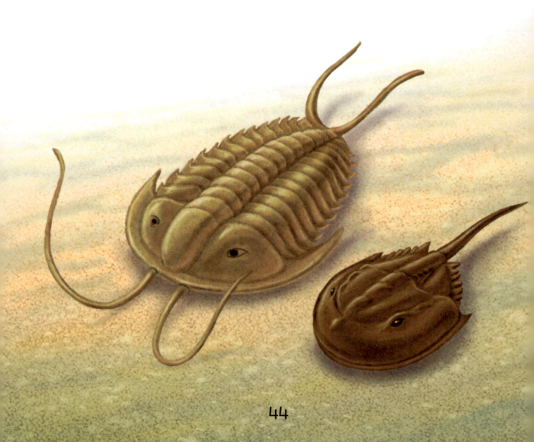

Trilobites scurried around and sucked food into their mouths like vacuum cleaners. They lived for 300 million years before they died out.

Early humans who lived before us sometimes made necklaces out of trilobite fossils. *Fossils* are rocks in the shape of a dead creature.

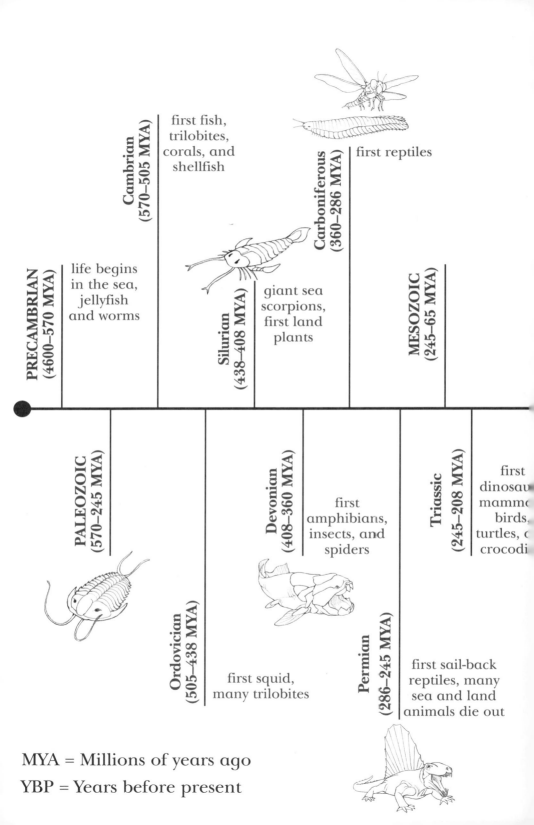

MYA = Millions of years ago
YBP = Years before present

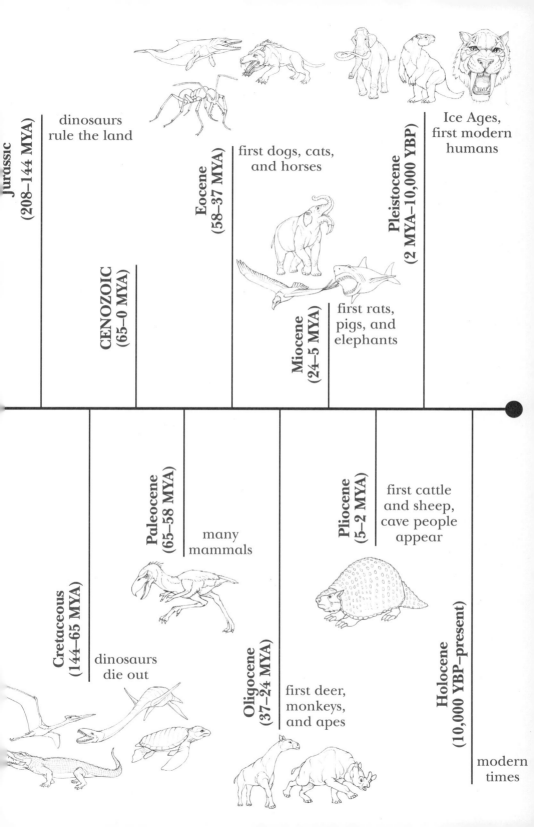

These gigantic creatures from the past are all *extinct*. That means they are all gone. But many animals alive today look like ones from long ago. Do you know this animal? It is an armadillo—to the max!